BLESS THIS MARRIAGE

GLORIA GAITHER

COUNTRYMAN

Published by J. Countryman, a division of Thomas Nelson Inc., Nashville, Tennessee

Project Editor—Terri Gibbs

A J. Countryman Book

Designed by Left Coast Design Inc.
Portland, Oregon

ISBN: 0-8499-5383-9

Printed and bound in Belgium

FOREWORD

*I*t is not good that man should be alone." And God Himself solved this problem by creating, unique in all creation, a partner for man—not of the dust of the earth, as was every other creature including man, but from an eternal being.

Weddings in Scripture were occasions of rich gifts, sumptuous feasting, and exquisite clothing. The bride's name was changed and the blessing of parents and those who were committed to being "community" for the couple was seriously and joyfully bestowed.

It is my deep and passionate desire that weddings find their way once again to the place of sacred importance that reflects the significance, permanence, and deep joy that marriage can and must possess if the human race is to survive physically, spiritually, and psychologically.

This significance must be recaptured by us, who make up the community of faith. We must train our children to value virtues and treasure true character so that they will be and look for marriage partners of quality. We, ourselves, must keep our promises and fulfill our commitments to give our children a model of what marriage and home can look and feel like.

And we must be there for couples who marry, not just at the wedding but all along their journey, to lift, support, encourage, nurture, and at times comfort, reminding them of their vows and our belief that problems should and can be solved. May we never forget that God Himself has pronounced marriage *honorable* (Heb. 13:5), *intimate* (Matt. 19:5), and *permanent* (Matt. 19:6).

Gloria Gaither

We, your friends and family, gather on this your wedding day to bless and celebrate with you the Holy Sacrament that will make you husband and wife.

he friends and family of
the bride represent a social history
and a genealogy that has brought
to this day this woman.

*H*er physical beauty, her unique personality, her memories and her dreams have been shaped and nurtured by the community of those gathered as "friends and family of the bride."

This man, on the other hand, has become what and who he is largely because of those gathered as the "friends and family of the groom."

They have profoundly influenced his aspirations, his mannerisms, his tastes and expectations, his spiritual and emotional maturity, and his psychological makeup.

*I*n part, it is your

similarities that have drawn

you together . . .

similar interests,

similar goals,

a shared faith.

*I*n part, it is your differences that have attracted you to each other.

*Y*ou inspire one another because

what one seems to lack, the other

seems to possess . . .

    where one of you seems weak,

    the other seems strong,

        when one seems reticent,

        the other seems confident.

*T*oday you stand at this altar because

of what you do and do not possess . . .

and because of two communities of

people who love you and have

poured what they had to bring

into your lives.

What brings us here today is ordained by God, whose Holy Word mandates that you step out from your two separate worlds and become one entity, "one flesh."

Apart from God, what we have come to celebrate would be impossible.

It will require a divine miracle.

*O*nly the God who created each of you,

as unique from all the world as a snowflake

on a silver breeze, could make of you two,

one abiding union strong enough to weather

the storms of life and not be torn apart.

*I*t is that mystical bonding that we have come to witness and to bless.

*A*part from birth and death and
your birth into the family of God,
this is the most holy and important
day of your lives.

*T*his sacrament of marriage is Holy Ground. It must not be taken lightly, for marriage is not a contract but a holy, three-way covenant between a man and a woman and God Himself.

$\mathcal{W}$e who have come to
witness and to bless this union
are also responsible to support,
to encourage, and, when the hard
times come (as they do to all
marriages) to remind you of this
vow to cherish with love,
to live in honor,
and to be faithful to each other
as long as you both shall live.

*I*t is our hope and expectation that you will walk together in the light of God's Word and in the bond of His love.

Only this bond will be strong enough to hold you secure when the storms come.

*D*raw your love for each other
from God's love for you.

Only that love is a source so deep
and inexhaustible that you need never
find yourselves empty of love,
no matter how much is demanded of you.

Your love for each other has singled you out and drawn your attention like a magnet away from all other attractions to focus on each other.

*N*ow may your love—

intensified and purified by this

sacrament—turn your attention

to focus outside yourselves.

May you find that love is fed and

multiplied by giving itself away.

*M*ay your physical union bring you great delight and be blessed with children to love and nurture—to call from you the best that is in you.

$\mathcal{M}$ay the union of your minds produce great ideas. Together, may you discover revelations of eternal truth.

May you never allow your thoughts to be spent on smallness, mediocrity, or regret.

*M*ay your social union bring
together around your table and hearth,
friends you each have known
and treasure.

May this circle continue to

widen as your home becomes a safe

and joyful center of warmth

and celebration.

May strong and secure ties
of trust grow between you and give
you the freedom to welcome the
hurt, the lonely, the broken,
and the stranger into the embrace
of your home.

*M*ay the security you feel in each others' embrace keep you from jealousy.

May you never feel threatened or abandoned when, for a time, you extend a hand of mercy or a heart of compassion to someone lost in the night.

*M*ay the union of your spirits
produce a shared hunger for the
presence of God in your home,
a shared appreciation for beauty,
and a longing for those
things that feed the
spirit—
great literature, art,
nature, and truth.

$\mathcal{M}$ay you yield to each

other freely . . .

your bodies,

your minds,

your social heritage,

and your spirits.

*M*ay your marriage draw you
ever closer to the heart of God,
give you complete satisfaction,
and bring you deep,
abiding joy in the love
you share together . . .
forever.

JOINED TOGETHER FOREVER

Groom's full name _____ OPOKU ACHEAMPONG

Bride's full name _____ MARY THERES YAA NUKUTELE

Date of Wedding _____ 13 – 98

Place of Wedding _____ WORD OF LIFE ASSEMBLY OF G

Members of the wedding party _____ CRYSTAL, KENNY
JEAN, KIM, SONYA, KRISTEN
SOLOMON, KWESI, GEORGE

Minister (priest) _____ REV D. WENDELL CLUVER